DISCARDED

HOSTAGE RESCUERS

Jamie Poolos

New York

Published in 2007 by The Rosen Publishing Group, Inc.
29 East 21st Street, New York, NY 10010

Copyright © 2007 by The Rosen Publishing Group, Inc.

First Edition

All rights reserved. No part of this book may be reproduced in any form without permission in writing from the publisher, except by a reviewer.

Library of Congress Cataloging-in-Publication Data

Poolos, Jamie.
Hostage rescuers / Jamie Poolos.
p. cm. — (Extreme careers)
Includes bibliographical references and index.
ISBN-13: 978-1-4042-0941-1
ISBN-10: 1-4042-0941-7 (library binding)
1. Hostages—Juvenile literature. 2. Rescues—Juvenile literature. 3. United States. Federal Bureau of Investigation. Hostage Rescue Team—Juvenile literature. I. Title.
HV6571.P66 2007
363.2'3—dc22

2006018442

Manufactured in the United States of America

On the cover: Dallas police SWAT members carry a girl from an apartment building after she was released by an armed man during a standoff in Dallas, Texas Wednesday November 12, 2003.

Contents

	Introduction	4
1	Teamwork	6
2	Training and Skills	20
3	Becoming a Hostage Negotiator	31
4	The Rescue Process	39
	Glossary	54
	For More Information	56
	For Further Reading	58
	Bibliography	60
	Index	62

Introduction

An enraged gunman has stormed into a downtown office building and taken hostages. A bank robber pinned down by Special Weapons and Tactics (SWAT) team officers wants to exchange a bank teller for a getaway car. A distraught man has barricaded himself in his house and is holding his wife and child at gunpoint. You may have seen live news reports on such tense standoffs with police that took hours, or even days, to diffuse. When desperate times call for desperate measures, only specially trained negotiators have the technical experience to help hostages.

Despite what you may think, whole teams of negotiators walk a fine line when dealing with hostage situations. It's not just sensitive psychologists with bullhorns and the innate ability to connect with desperate

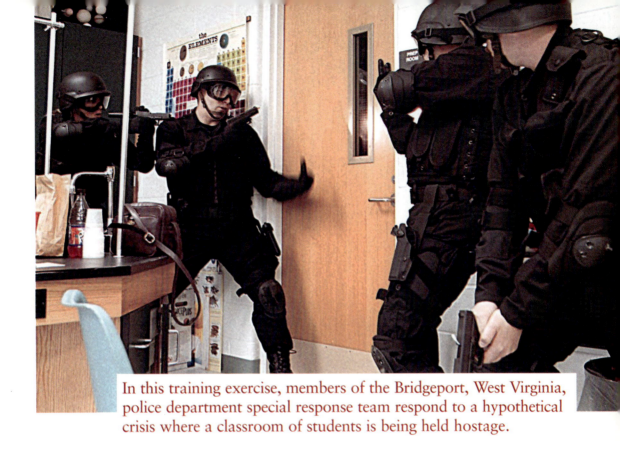

In this training exercise, members of the Bridgeport, West Virginia, police department special response team respond to a hypothetical crisis where a classroom of students is being held hostage.

criminals. Negotiation teams are usually made up of uniformed soldiers or police personnel wearing flak jackets and toting assault rifles. Hostage negotiators are men and women who have undergone countless hours of training in weapons handling, entry tactics, negotiations, psychology, and criminal behavior. They perform the physically, mentally, and emotionally exhausting work necessary to bring potentially violent situations to peaceful resolutions.

Teamwork

In order to understand the hostage negotiator's duties, as well as the techniques he or she employs, it is helpful to consider the mind-set of those who take hostages. For as long as anyone can remember, criminals have been taking hostages to get what they want. According to the *Hostage Negotiation Study Guide*, developed by the International Association of Chiefs of Police and the Federal Law Enforcement Training Center, "Hostage taking has occurred throughout recorded history, including ancient Greek, Norse, and Roman mythologies." Recently, the war in Iraq has brought attention to hostage taking, as Western journalists and civilian workers are often held by people who make unreasonable demands.

But political events are not the only context in which hostage taking is used as a tactic. Criminals and cult leaders have all used hostages as bargaining chips. Some have taken family members hostage. Hostage situations have occurred in private businesses and in government offices. Even students have been held captive in universities and high schools.

Motivation

According to the *Hostage Negotiation Study Guide*, criminals take hostages through "well-planned or spontaneous reactions to a situation." Criminals may take hostages when they are trapped in order to use them as a way to bargain their way out of a dangerous situation. Disturbed persons may take hostages to draw attention to their complaints or demands.

Antisocial groups, like cults, have also been known to spontaneously hold members hostage when threatened by outside forces. Terrorists and other political and religious groups usually take hostages as part of their plan or agenda. Leaders of these fringe groups often take hostages to draw attention to their cause and demoralize people who oppose their political or moral viewpoint.

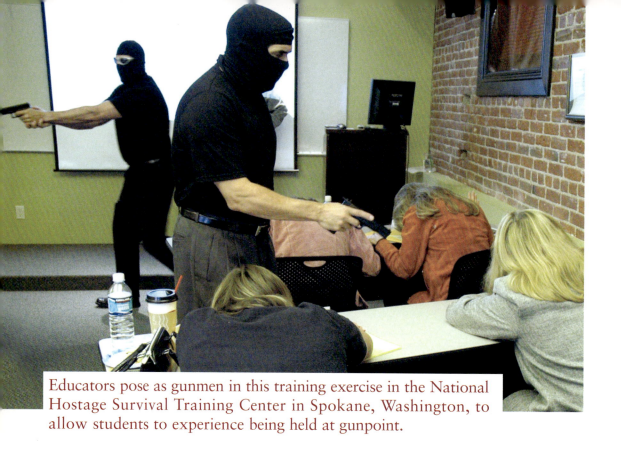

Educators pose as gunmen in this training exercise in the National Hostage Survival Training Center in Spokane, Washington, to allow students to experience being held at gunpoint.

Typically, spontaneous hostage takers intend to use hostages to ensure their own individual survival. In such cases, the criminal may lack the conviction to actually harm the hostages, who he or she only took in haste. On the other hand, premeditated hostage taking often involves criminals who are armed with guns or explosives. They are commonly willing to die or be killed for the sake or survival of their cause or distorted beliefs.

Because there are so many situations in which innocent people are captured, hostage negotiators are necessary in all areas of law enforcement, on both the domestic and international levels. Negotiators play roles in local police departments, Special Weapons and Tactics (SWAT) teams, the Federal Bureau of Investigation (FBI), the Secret Service, and the Central Intelligence Agency (CIA).

Metropolitan Special Response Teams

To successfully increase the safe release of hostages, negotiators work in teams or units. Individuals on these teams undergo training above and beyond the standards required of typical police personnel. Hostage negotiation multipurpose teams are an increasingly important part of local law enforcement agencies, like your local police department. One example of an active and successful unit is the Metro-Dade Police Department in Florida, which deploys a special response team (SRT) consisting of nearly thirty officers who have undergone SWAT training that includes hostage rescue skills.

A mock riot is staged at Moundsville State Penitentiary, a Civil War-era prison, to give officers a chance to practice methods of controlling people during a variety of situations.

According to supervisors at the Metro-Dade Police Department, SRT officers respond to approximately 400 operations a year, some of which involve hostage rescue. Although a pair of lieutenants officially commands the team, sergeants supervise the officers, who work each day and rotate in teams of three to cover nights and weekends. Personnel are both disciplined and motivated, but the emphasis is on teamwork, not superhuman athleticism or hotshot shooting skills. More than anything

Teamwork

else, SRT officers must be disciplined enough to follow a plan without changing the rules on a whim.

Even so, many municipalities are unable to divert extra funding to train officers and teams for hostage negotiation. Even those cities whose police departments feature trained hostage negotiators often turn to federal law enforcement when faced with an emergency of such magnitude as a hostage situation. In those incidences, local police have the option of calling on the FBI, which is available to serve and assist local law enforcement agencies. FBI agents have undergone even more specialized training than local law enforcement officers.

Federal Bureau of Investigation

The purpose of the FBI is to protect and defend the United States against terrorist and foreign intelligence threats, to uphold and enforce the criminal laws of the United States, and to provide leadership and criminal justice services to federal, state, municipal, and international agencies and partners. The organization has more than 450 field and satellite offices, and it is always

In this photograph, an FBI hostage rescue team is lowered from a helicopter during a practice demonstration at the FBI Training Academy in Quantico, Virginia.

searching for new recruits with the desire for extreme challenges. The FBI motto, "Fidelity, Bravery, and Integrity," shares the same first letters of the organization whose members swear to uphold those convictions.

The FBI's original hostage rescue team was created in 1982 as a security precaution for the Olympic Games in Los Angeles. It operated as a stand-alone unit for more than a decade. By 1994, the FBI founded a tactical support branch, called the Critical Incident Response

Group (CIRG). This group was composed of a hostage rescue team and an operations training unit that worked together as one. Today, the CIRG is ready to protect Americans both at home and overseas. As a part of the CIRG, the hostage rescue team serves primarily as a domestic counterterrorism unit that seeks "tactical resolution option[s] in hostage and high-risk law enforcement situations."

The hostage rescue teams of the FBI are made up of carefully selected agents who are both experienced and extraordinarily motivated. Originally, this division of the FBI had fifty operators, but today's members number four times that amount. All of them are trained on-site at FBI headquarters in Quantico, Virginia. Hostage rescue team members are qualified FBI special agents who have successfully completed a demanding and rigorous two-week tryout and have volunteered to become part of the hostage negotiation team. Volunteers are selected based on their background and experience.

Once selected, they undergo four months of additional training at the FBI Academy by the Operations Training Unit (OTU). The OTU has access to Special Forces instructors and is a valuable component that helps ensure that FBI hostage rescuers are prepared to meet any number of serious crisis situations. Details of the OTU's training curriculum are largely classified, however.

FBI Hostage Rescue Team Mission

FBI hostage rescue team members are considered among the most highly trained and best-equipped tactical operators in the world. They sometimes train with international Special Forces units, like the United States' Delta Force and France's Group d'Intervention de la Gendarmerie Nationale (GIGN).

The team's mission is to deploy within four hours of assignment and rescue people who are being held illegally by hostile criminals and terrorists. They help protect U.S. citizens from terrorist attacks and support all levels of law enforcement officers. These special agents are trained to encounter a variety of heated situations, both within the United States and internationally, including combating cyber-based attacks and high-technology crimes.

These highly specialized, tactical law enforcement operations may include:

An FBI special agent points his weapon at a video screen during a 2001 demonstration of the agency's interactive firearms training system in Los Angeles, California.

- Hostage rescue and barricaded subjects
- High-risk arrests
- Manhunts in rural environments
- Helicopter operations
- Locating weapons of mass destruction

The FBI's hostage rescue team has been deployed on more than 200 occasions, most often in support of FBI criminal and terrorist investigations. In addition to

Hostage Rescuers

hostage rescue, these missions include barricaded subjects, high-risk arrest and warrant raids, dive search, hurricane relief operations, dignitary protection (such as presidential inaugurations), and protection for large special events (such as the Olympic Games).

Hostage negotiators are found in all levels of law enforcement, from local to international. They work in teams that respond to diverse hostile situations, only some of which involve hostages.

International Hostage Rescue

Internationally, hostage rescuers are usually part of counterterrorist units, which perform a multitude of extremely specialized operations. Counterterrorist units operate within unique guidelines such as those imposed by groups like Delta Force. These units are composed of elite soldiers trained in the most advanced, cutting-edge military and psychological tactics. They are called upon when political negotiations become ineffective and a favorable resolution can come only by the use of force.

Fully explaining the activities involved in training Special Forces operators can easily fill several books. In

This photograph shows the release of four hostages in 2002 during a raid of a Moscow theater. Chechen gunmen held 900 people for two days demanding withdrawal of Russian forces from Chechnya.

short, international counterterrorist personnel are selected from the best recruits the armed forces have to offer. The challenge associated with the selection of these officers is rigorous and demanding, both physically and mentally. Only the best members of the army, marines, navy, and air force are offered the chance to qualify. Training is continual and grueling. An emphasis is placed on perfecting techniques, as well as innovating tactics and equipment that will aid both international and domestic agencies. In international hostage rescue situations, terrorists are typically willing to sacrifice their own lives in addition to the lives of others in order to promote their causes. Therefore, Special Forces personnel are trained to kill these terrorists rather than employ traditional negotiation techniques. When conducting raids to free hostages, whether the hostages are civilians, downed pilots, or other armed forces personnel, these individuals are trained to shoot first and ask questions later.

Private Hostage Rescue Services

With the increase of business ventures in hostile countries such as Afghanistan and Iraq, civilian hostage negotiation has become a growing field. Recently, civilian hostages have been taken by hostile governments or splinter military organizations in Afghanistan, Iraq, Iran, and parts of Africa. As a result, large corporations, like oil companies and insurance providers, may employ their own hostage negotiators. Typically, these individuals have received their training in the FBI and/or Special Forces, and they may have completed military or law enforcement careers.

Teamwork

    Because the nature of hostage negotiation in foreign countries is drastically different from the negotiation process at home, this book will not explore careers in Special Forces. Instead, it will focus on careers in hostage negotiation with domestic law enforcement agencies.

Training and Skills

When a criminal takes hostages and threatens to kill them if his demands are not met, law enforcement and government agents are faced with difficult decisions. It has never been the practice of the police or the FBI to surrender to the demands of hostage takers. At the same time, the safety of the hostages remains a top priority. These situations require teams of highly trained personnel who will disable or kill the taker without harming the hostages.

Training is a key part of the negotiator's career. Whether they're FBI or local law enforcement, hostage rescuers must undergo countless hours of specialized training in a wide variety of disciplines. These include weapons and tactics, negotiation, behavioral psychology, and communications.

Members of the Connecticut Capital Region Emergency Services Team in East Hartford, Connecticut, enter an armored vehicle in 2003 in response to a reported murder-suicide in the area.

Municipal Hostage Rescue Teams

Many municipal hostage rescue teams receive training from private organizations and state associations. Groups such as the Public Agency Training Council (PATC), a private company that trains law enforcement agencies; the International Association of Hostage Negotiators; and the Florida Association of Hostage Negotiators offer seminars in particular aspects of hostage negotiation, tactics, and weapons training. Former members of the armed forces, FBI, and municipal police departments usually teach these seminars, which typically last from one to two weeks. Participants can expect to spend time in a classroom setting, listening to experts describe procedures and strategies, watching videotapes, and acting out various crisis scenarios. Other courses are based solely on role-playing and scenario modeling, so participants can apply what they have learned in a way that involves accurate movement, timing, and the manipulation of gear and arms. In these scenarios, participants conduct operations against "enemy" hostage takers (usually with full gear but dummy ammunition) to get a real sense of what it's like to make decisions and take actions while under tremendous stress. Instructors and peers then evaluate the methods of the participants to improve their techniques. Programs emphasize physical and mental preparedness, safety techniques, team-building exercises, risk assessment, and tactics for approaching hostage takers and for entering buildings and rooms where hostages are being held.

As you might imagine, a number of different scenarios are studied, discussed, and reenacted as courses and seminars. These scenarios model the typically intense situations faced by hostage rescuers, who must constantly develop and hone their tactics, techniques, and communication skills to be as prepared as possible. Some courses and seminars include the following:

Negotiations in Correctional Settings

Each year, there are violent uprisings in federal and state prisons throughout the United States. Violent criminals with the grim prospect of life imprisonment can be difficult partners in negotiation. These hostage takers are considered some of the most volatile. They are typically able to lock themselves and their hostages into highly secure rooms of the prison, often with plenty of provisions to hold out for weeks or even months. Their hostages are almost always prison guards and/or other inmates.

Negotiating with Jumpers

Individuals with suicidal tendencies may often position themselves on bridges, on rooftops, or at windows as they

The New York Police Department officers in this photograph reason with a man who is considering jumping from the fourth floor of a Manhattan building.

struggle with thoughts of ending their lives. These people are consumed with feelings of desperation and grief. Because their decision to put themselves in such a precarious situation is frequently the result of snap judgments, negotiators are often successful in "talking them down."

Risk Assessment and Response

While the well-equipped law enforcement officers on the ground draw the most attention during hostage

Training and Skills

rescues, the men and women who plan the rescue operation deserve much of the credit. Commanders and team leaders are trained to address the tactical considerations for emergency response operations. They must use this training, coupled with their experience, to assess the danger of a situation. They must also assess the risks associated with each strategy and tactic at their disposal. Considerations include the safety of the team, the general public, the hostage or hostages, and the taker, and the potential destruction of private property.

A Focus on Psychology

In addition to receiving physical and tactical training in the form of scenarios, hostage rescuers are trained to identify and assess various levels of risk. This means that they must learn to identify and respond to certain behaviors a hostage taker exhibits that may indicate his likelihood of harming the hostage or himself, or of putting the team in danger. More experienced rescuers study negotiation techniques to help bring these situations to a peaceful end.

Hostage Rescuers

Team Readiness

Another important area of training is preparation for rapid response. Commanders must ensure that their teams are ready to act at a moment's notice. In addition, commanders must be trained to deal with media coverage of crisis situations, particularly during ongoing struggles. Saying the right thing at the right time can help keep the public informed without causing panic or compromising the operation. It's also important to represent the team and the entire chain of command as competent, highly trained professionals.

Special Equipment and Clothing

Hostage rescuers require precision equipment to ensure their safety and the safety of others. With the exception of sniper rifles, telescopic sights, and surveillance equipment such as cameras and binoculars, most of the gear is designed for close-quarter combat. Units across the country use any variation of the following items, which are part of rescuers' basic equipment:

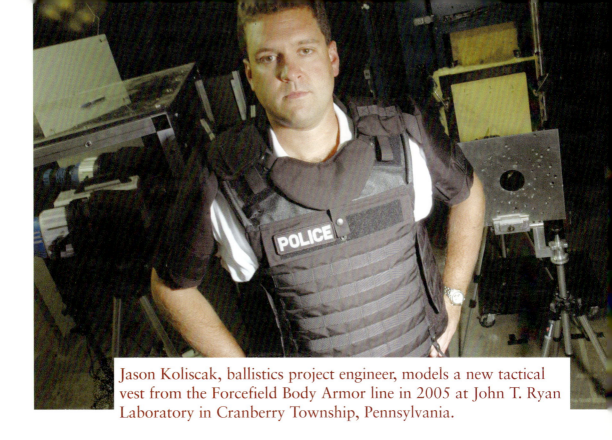

Jason Koliscak, ballistics project engineer, models a new tactical vest from the Forcefield Body Armor line in 2005 at John T. Ryan Laboratory in Cranberry Township, Pennsylvania.

- Flame-resistant coveralls and gloves
- Bulletproof body armor vest
- Outer tactical vest with pockets to hold and organize gear
- Bulletproof Kevlar helmet
- Balaclava (a hood that covers the face)
- Goggles to protect the eyes
- Gas mask to guard against the effects of tear gas and other chemicals
- Soft-soled boots for silent movement

Hostage Rescuers

Weapons

Hostage rescuers require specific clothing and gear for protection, and they must be armed. The following is a list of some of the most commonly used weapons:

Submachine guns: Favored for use in close-combat situations where short bursts of fire are required, submachine guns such as the 9mm Heckler and Koch MP5 are commonly used by officers employed by law enforcement agencies and the military.

Assault rifles: All-purpose, automatic rifles such as the M16 are standard issue in many U.S. law enforcement agencies.

Shotguns: Along with submachine guns, shotguns are favored for use in close-combat situations where a spray of ammunition is required. Hostage rescuers also use shotguns to demolish door hinges when there is insufficient room to use a battering ram.

Sniper rifles: These precision weapons are used for long-range situations. Snipers are often placed on rooftops or in windows outside of the hostage taker's area of focus. Popular sniper rifles are the M116A4 and the Russian-made SVD Dragunov.

Handguns: Semi-automatic, personal firearms are used when maximum mobility is required or in cramped spaces where rifles are too cumbersome. The M9 is a popular handgun used by law enforcement officers.

Tear gas grenades: Tear gas is used to immobilize a target or to flush the target from his or her barricade.

Flexi-cuffs: Lightweight, plastic handcuffs that are similar to zip-ties, Flexi-cuffs are easier to carry and lighter than traditional metal handcuffs.

Other Tools

Part of any hostage rescue team's arsenal are tools for observation and reconnaissance. Much can be learned

A member of a Greek police anti-terrorism team puts on night vision goggles as part of a readiness exercise at the Amigdaleza Police Academy near Athens, Greece, in 2003.

about a hostage taker by watching and studying his behavior from a safe distance. Teams use binoculars, fiber-optic cameras, and night-vision goggles to keep an eye on criminals and their activity. Whenever possible, rescue teams employ the use of helicopters to gain a bird's-eye view of the environment. FBI and SWAT personnel also use armored cars and vans.

Becoming a Hostage Negotiator

In the early morning of January 18, 2004, two prison cellmates, Ricky Wassenaar and Steven Coy, took command of the kitchen and eventually a guard tower at the Arizona State Prison Complex in Lewis, Arizona. Their actions set in motion the longest prison hostage standoff in U.S. history. It lasted for fifteen days, until a team of negotiators and law enforcement agents from sixteen departments worked together to negotiate surrender.

Kip Rustenburg, a sergeant in the Maricopa County Sheriff's Office, had just over a year's experience as a negotiator and seven incidents under her belt. She was pushed into the role of lead negotiator. In *Anatomy of a Hostage Negotiation*, by John D. Baker, Rustenburg explained why leading negotiations is her passion:

A Department of Public Safety helicopter shuttles SWAT officers to the Arizona State Prison Complex-Lewis in Buckeye, Arizona, to subdue a hostage crisis there in January 2004.

I work best under extreme situations. I can't think of a more extreme situation than what I just went through; [it's] such an adrenaline rush. And when it happens, and it's good, it's like I really made a difference . . . a man is alive because of me.

No matter the type of hostage situation, police commanders are generally faced with four options to contain and control it. After officers arrive on the scene, they may be ordered to use massive firepower and assault. The second option is to use selective sniper fire. The third is to force the hostage taker out with chemical agents. The final option is to contain the area and negotiate with the taker by employing a specially trained negotiator. The first three options will almost always result in injuries or fatalities.

To avoid injuries, police commanders often first attempt to employ the use of negotiators to diffuse a hostile situation. Negotiation remains one of the most important tactics. Whether or not the hostage or hostage takers live through the conflict often depends exclusively on the negotiation process.

Hostage negotiation is a demanding, high-stress, and sometimes dangerous profession. Before an individual is hired for this duty, he or she must master the basics. Typically, the foundation of a negotiator's career is based on several years as a law enforcement officer, usually as part of a police force or FBI. During this time, the future hostage rescuer gains the excessive training and experience he or she needs with weapons, capabilities, and procedure. This is also the time when he or she will learn how to handle a variety of crisis situations. More important, several years as an officer or agent will give him or her experience in negotiating with people during hostile and desperate situations. Lieutenant Gary Schmidt of the Cheektowaga Police Department in Cheektowaga, New York, said in *How Hostage Negotiation Works*:

> You hone your skills as an officer because you talk to people all the time. A lot of the people you talk to, while not in an 'official crisis,' are in some kind of crisis situation. You learn a lot just from active listening and interacting with people.

General Requirements

In order to become a police officer or FBI agent, you must satisfy certain physical and psychological criteria. Since education and training is continual, you have to absorb information and immediately apply what you've learned. The physical training is also demanding because officers and agents are expected to confront criminals of all sizes, as well as maintain mental alertness over long periods.

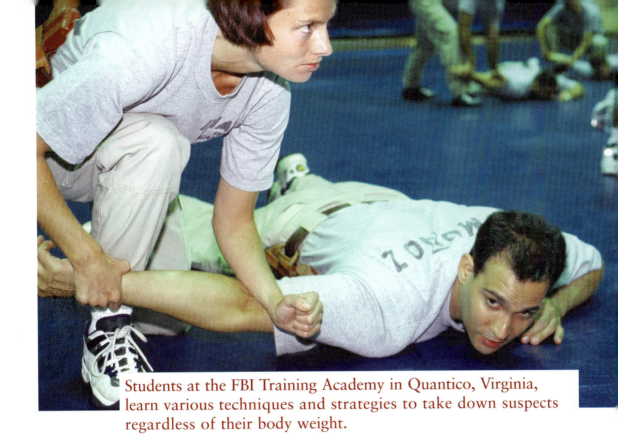

Students at the FBI Training Academy in Quantico, Virginia, learn various techniques and strategies to take down suspects regardless of their body weight.

The FBI's requirements are even more stringent. An individual must possess a bachelor's degree from an accredited college. The degree must be in law, accounting, science, or languages. The individual must also pass a criminal background check and vision tests proving that at least one eye has perfect 20/20 vision. Applicants then undergo an intensive, four-month initial training period at FBI headquarters in Quantico, Virginia, before they are eligible for placement.

A career as a hostage negotiator requires an immense sense of responsibility and the fortitude to withstand a stressful day-to-day existence. Anyone who is placed on a metropolitan police force or in the FBI must understand that there are some instances when he or she will be ordered to shoot to kill. To save the most lives, hostage negotiators must understand the motivation for, and consequences of, violent actions.

Working as a FBI agent or SWAT team member teaches you how to handle weapons and offers experience in settling hostage situations. However, you must undergo additional training if you want a career as a hostage negotiator. Usually, this means you must take courses in psychology and learn to deal with people who are emotionally volatile or unstable. This means learning about various personality types and personality disorders.

Organizations such as the Public Agency Training Council and the International Association of Hostage Negotiators offer seminars and training courses for future negotiators. Some take university courses in behavioral psychology. A negotiator's education is ongoing throughout his or her career.

Learning the ropes as an FBI officer or hostage negotiator requires plenty of lecture classes in traditional settings on subjects as varied as law, psychology, ballistics, forensics, and criminology.

Selection

Some police departments do not have a formal process for selecting officers who would make good hostage negotiators. If faced with an immediate need to fill this specific role, department heads normally select applicants based on training and experience. Top applicants are considered outstanding if they relate well to people and have an innate desire to help during conflicts. Other necessary qualities are levelheadedness and the ability to work as part of a team. If you're an approachable person who naturally sets people at ease, you may be an excellent hostage negotiator.

Once selected, applicants undergo a series of interviews and tests, some of which include role-playing in scenarios they could face on the job. Examples are suicides and bank robberies where children are taken hostage. Selection committees evaluate applicants based on their performance, namely how they handle the situations, how calm they remain, and how they balance the checklists of appropriate responses with their own creative solutions. Successful applicants will typically complete a one-week, forty-hour intensive course on hostage negotiation strategies and tactics.

The Rescue Process

Because hostage situations can be unpredictable, hostage rescuers require extensive training. Of vital importance is the fact that innocent civilians are placed in extreme danger. Unlike a terrorist strike with the detonation of a bomb, hostage situations allow law enforcement agencies the opportunity to rescue civilians. A straightforward, armed confrontation can be risky. The negotiation process is the most crucial part of any such crisis. A negotiator must find out who the hostage taker is, what he wants, and what it will take to achieve a peaceful outcome—all while ensuring the safety of everyone involved. This chapter describes the basic negotiation process and some of the techniques used to diffuse hostage situations.

Most domestic hostage conflicts are motivated by the personal needs of the hostage takers. These needs

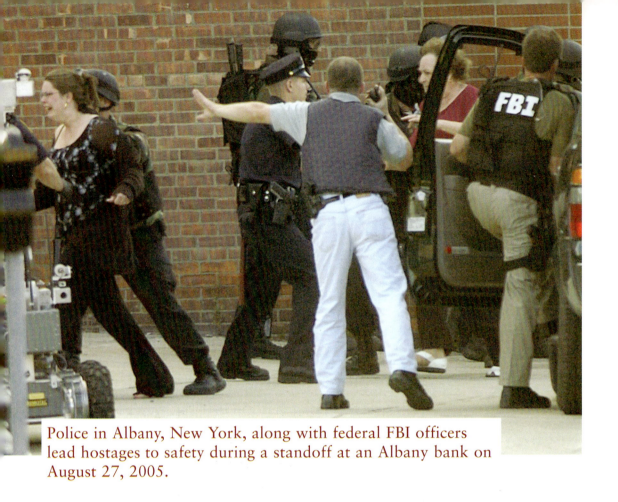

Police in Albany, New York, along with federal FBI officers lead hostages to safety during a standoff at an Albany bank on August 27, 2005.

include the desire for safe passage, wanting to settle a personal grievance like getting back at a former employer, or calling attention to a political cause like student war protesters taking university officials hostage. In many cases, the hostages become human shields or bargaining chips used to ensure the safety of the hostage taker while he attempts to escape.

Stages of a Hostage Crisis

Most hostage situations unfold in three phases. In the initial phase, the crime of abduction occurs and the hostage taker makes his demands. In the second phase, law enforcement officials attempt to engage the taker in a conversation. This phase can last for hours, as in the case of a bank robbery gone wrong. Or it can take weeks, like the case of Ruby Ridge, where a deadly ten-day shootout took place in Idaho between the Weaver family and government agents in 1992. In the third and final phase, the hostage taker either surrenders or faces the consequence of an assault by law enforcement agents. (Occasionally, the taker's demands are met and he escapes, but this is rare.)

Once a hostage situation is reported, police, local crisis teams, and possibly the FBI are deployed. Officers effectively surround the site, cutting off any possible escape route. At this point, the negotiation phase begins. The negotiator attempts to establish contact with the hostage taker and determine why he has taken hostages. If the negotiator is able to establish contact, he

Hostage Rescuers

Attorney William Kunstler *(right)* negotiates with prison inmates who have taken other inmates hostage inside the Attica State Correctional Facility in 1971 after killing nine prison employees.

or she will assess the mental and emotional state of the taker and communicate risk indicators to the entire team.

The two principal members of any hostage negotiation team are the commander, who oversees all operations, and the negotiator, who is the liaison between the hostage taker, the law enforcement agency, and sometimes the

The Rescue Process

hostages. The primary task of this phase is information gathering. Officers report to the commander from their positions. Others run background checks on the hostage taker. The negotiator will attempt to establish a line of communication with the taker to determine his reasons for taking hostages, as well as his demands. If there is

Hostage Rescuers

more than one hostage taker, then the negotiator must establish a dialogue with the leader. Due to extensive training, a negotiator knows what questions will provide the most crucial information. Through the hostage taker's responses—and through his mannerisms and tone of voice—the negotiator can begin to form his or her psychological profile.

The negotiator will evaluate this psychological profile to determine the hostage taker's ultimate intentions. The negotiator may characterize the taker as emotionally unstable, calculating and deliberate, experienced or inexperienced, or suicidal or hopeful. The negotiator will also try to determine the condition of those held captive—the number of hostages and how many are wounded or dead. Meanwhile, other team members gather information about the crime scene, like the building's floor plan and escape routes, and who may have a clear shot at the taker, should shooting be necessary.

Principles of Hostage Negotiation

The longer a hostage situation lasts, the greater the possibility for a safe outcome. Yet sometimes, this isn't

Flames engulf the Branch Davidian compound on April 19, 1993, in Waco, Texas. Eighty-one Davidians, including leader David Koresh, perished as federal agents tried to drive the group out.

the case. In 1993, officers from the Bureau of Alcohol, Tobacco, and Firearms raided Mt. Carmel Center in Waco, Texas, where a group of cult members known as Branch Davidians remained secluded on their compound for fifty-one days. The initial raid resulted in the deaths of four agents and five Davidians. When no peaceful accord could be reached, the compound was set ablaze, killing seventy-six more people. To this day, the identity of who set the fire remains unknown.

Hostage Rescuers

To increase the likelihood of a positive resolution, negotiators use stall tactics to extend the conflict whenever possible. These tactics may include insisting that they cannot make decisions or guarantees without consulting superiors and asking the hostage taker to give specifics regarding his demands.

Negotiators work to steer the situation in their favor by following guidelines. The first priority is to ensure the safety of all hostages by encouraging their safe release. A common tactic is to plead for the release of children, the elderly, and anyone who is injured or pregnant. Sometimes, the negotiator can convince the hostage taker that an armed assault is imminent and that he can buy more time by releasing people. On other occasions, the negotiator will provide food and water in exchange for a hostage's safe release. When a hostage is released, he or she is medically treated if necessary, then immediately interviewed. Hostages can provide invaluable information about the exact position of their abductor and his psychological state.

The second principle is to maintain an air of calm. Obviously, anyone who is desperate enough to threaten the lives of others needs to be handled with caution.

Hostage takers are not only aggravated, they are also filled with adrenaline. Factor in the potential psychological instability of the taker and his belief that violence is acceptable, and any aggressive behavior on the negotiator's part could result in disaster. The negotiator must convey a sense of calm through his or her tone of voice. Negotiators are trained never to argue or to say no to a taker's demands. Instead, they use stall tactics or make counteroffers.

The third principle is to establish and foster the relationship with the hostage taker. In essence, the negotiator becomes the taker's caregiver, providing supplies and possibly meeting small demands during the standoff. This makes the negotiator more credible and trustworthy. The negotiator also encourages the taker to see the hostages as human beings, usually by directing attention to their well-being through regular inquiries. At the same time, the negotiator tries to get the taker to see the broader picture beyond the immediate situation and to acknowledge that life is more meaningful than his immediate needs. If the negotiator is successful in creating a connection between the taker and his hostages, it becomes more difficult for the taker to kill.

A Police officer (*right*) leads a child away from a mall in Tacoma, Washington, during a crisis where an armed man took hostages shortly after noon on November 20, 2005.

This subtle process of maintaining control and establishing a relationship with the hostage taker demands patience, concentration, and adaptability. At the beginning of a hostage crisis, demands are often unreasonable and the taker is typically unwilling to negotiate. As the negotiator does his or her job, however, new information forces the negotiator to make a strategy adjustment. Often, the negotiator does not have the authority to meet the taker's demands, especially if these demands entail a large sum of money or the release of prisoners. Over time, the negotiator may make small concessions such as the supply of food, water, and comfort items. Sometimes, the negotiator will promise media coverage in exchange for one or more hostages or fewer demands. This establishes the role of the negotiator as one who won't typically give the taker exactly what he wants, but will give him something of value. Following this strategy, the negotiator can gradually weaken the taker's position.

Strategies

As the process unfolds, the commander looks for opportunities to intervene. One tactic is to lure the hostage taker out of the barricade to pick up supplies. In one scenario, the taker sends his lone hostage out to retrieve a pack of cigarettes the negotiator promised. At this point, a law officer motions to the hostage to run away, and the SWAT team can then move in to disarm the taker.

The following list is just a few strategies that were employed by successful negotiators to gradually wear down a hostage taker and take control of a situation:

- Take advantage of every moment to get the hostage taker to consider the finer points or subtleties of the situation.
- Ask open-ended questions, rather than yes/no questions, to encourage dialogue.
- Avoid confrontation. Instead, use negotiation tactics to solve problems.
- Get something in return for each demand met.
- Play to the hostage taker's sense of humanity. Convince him to release women and children and people with medical needs.
- Manipulate the taker's environment by controlling the electricity, phone, water, air-conditioning, and/or heating.
- Avoid negative responses. Instead of saying no, the negotiator should delay his or her response or explain that a supervisor must approve of his request.
- Be positive. The negotiator must convey the attitude that everything can be worked out, even if he or she has informed the entry team that it appears an entry will be needed.

The Rescue Process

- Do not give the taker the impression that the hostages are the most important concern, even though they are.
- Keep a record of milestones and setbacks in the negotiation process.
- Create situations in which takers and hostages must cooperate. This makes it more difficult for the taker to harm hostages. A common tactic is to provide food or drink in bulk so the taker and hostages must work together to prepare and serve it.

When determining appropriate strategies and tactics, the negotiator must take all of his or her knowledge of the situation into account. In some cases, hostage takers may be discouraged by a strong show of manpower, while others may react negatively to seeing a lot of uniformed law enforcement agents and vehicles with flashing lights.

The End Game

If a negotiator is successful, a hostage incident can have one of two outcomes: either the hostage taker surrenders,

Two hostage negotiators and a hostage *(left)* leave a Moscow theater where Chechen rebels held Russians captive for two days in 2002. Russian authorities later stormed the theater; 130 hostages and 42 Chechens were killed.

or law enforcement agents intervene to subdue or execute him. It is the job of the commander and the negotiator to determine if and when such an intervention occurs. If a sniper or assault team has clear access to the taker and can act with little risk to the hostages, and if negotiations are at a standstill, intervention is the logical choice. If the taker is determined to be volatile and the hostages appear to be in immediate danger, the commander may call for an assault. In such a case, tear gas may be used to disorient the taker while the assault team storms the barricade. Although this strategy puts the hostages in harm's way, it is often the best solution to minimize fatalities.

Hostage incidents in which no one is harmed are a credit to the entire rescue team, especially the negotiator. Every hostage incident serves as an education, no matter the outcome, so that future incidents can be resolved successfully.

Glossary

balaclava A woolen hood that covers the head.
ballistics The study of the firing, flight, and effects of ammunition.
capitulate To surrender under specified conditions; come to terms.
conviction A strong opinion or belief.
counterterrorism Intended to prevent or counteract terrorism.
credible Capable of being believed.
deploy To position troops for combat; to bring forces into action.
diffuse To spread about, or scatter or dilute.
domestic Of or relating to a country's internal affairs.
forensics The science and technology of investigating criminal acts.

Glossary

immersion To engage wholly; to become a part of something.

innate A natural ability, quality, or talent that a person has from birth.

intervention To involve oneself in a situation so as to alter or hinder an action or development.

Kevlar A tough, synthetic fabric that is used to make bullet-proof vests.

negotiate To settle by discussion and mutual agreement.

perpetrator One who is responsible for a crime.

personality disorder A psychological term that indicates that a person is emotionally unbalanced in some way, such as the result of a mood disorder or depression for instance.

premeditate To think out or plan an action or activity before carrying it out.

psychology The study of the human mind and its emotional behaviors.

subdue To bring under control; dominate.

tactics The military science that deals with securing objectives set by strategy, especially the technique of deploying and directing troops, ships, and aircraft in effective maneuvers against an enemy.

For More Information

Federal Bureau of Investigation (FBI)
J. Edgar Hoover Building
935 Pennsylvania Avenue NW
Washington, DC 20535-0001
(202) 324-3000
Web site: http://www.fbi.gov

Institute of Police Technology and Management
University of North Florida
12000 Alumni Drive
Jacksonville, FL 32224-2678
(904) 620-4786
Web site: http://www.iptm.org

For More Information

National Tactical Officers Association (NTOA)
P.O. Box 797
Doylestown, PA 18901
(800) 279-9127
Web site: http://www.ntoa.org

Western States Hostage Negotiators' Association
Seattle Police Department
2300 SW Webster Street
Seattle, WA 98106
Web site: http://www.wshna.org

Web Sites

Due to the changing nature of Internet links, Rosen Publishing has developed an online list of Web sites related to the subject of this book. This site is updated regularly. Please use this link to access the list:

http://www.rosenlinks.com/ec/hosre

For Further Reading

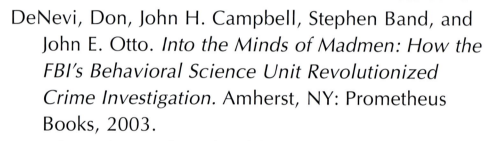

DeNevi, Don, John H. Campbell, Stephen Band, and John E. Otto. *Into the Minds of Madmen: How the FBI's Behavioral Science Unit Revolutionized Crime Investigation.* Amherst, NY: Prometheus Books, 2003.

Douglas, John, and Mark Olshaker. *The Anatomy of Motive: The FBI's Legendary Mindhunter Explores the Key to Understanding and Catching Violent Criminals.* New York, NY: Pocket Books, 2000.

Johnson, Leroy. *Hostage Rescue Manual.* Revised edition. London, England: Greenhill Books, 2005.

Kessler, Ronald. *The FBI: Inside the World's Most Powerful Law Enforcement Agency.* New York, NY: Pocket Books, 1994.

Koletar, Joseph. *The FBI Career Guide.* New York, NY: AMACOM, 2006.

For Further Reading

Louden, Robert J. *Crime and Justice in New York City.* New York, NY: McGraw Hill, 1998.

Thompson, Leroy. *Hostage Rescue Manual: Tactics of the Counter-Terrorist Professionals.* Mechanicsburg, PA: Stackpole Books, 2001.

Bibliography

Baker, John D. "Anatomy of a Hostage Negotiation: An Interview with a Primary Negotiator." *Negotiator Magazine.* August 2004. Retrieved February 1, 2006 (http://www.negotatiormagazine.com).

Caneva, Ed. "Metro Dade Police Department (Special Response Team)." Retrieved January 10, 2006 (http://www.specialoperations.com/Domestic/dadesrt.html).

"Counterterrorism: SWAT Operations, Tactics, Equipment, Training." Retrieved January 10, 2006 (http://www.specialoperations.com).

Counterterrorism and Hostage Rescue. "The Techniques." Retrieved January 6, 2006 (http://students.engr.scu.edu/~jabraham/specwar/specops/ct2.html).

Federal Bureau of Investigation. Investigative Programs Critical Incidents Response Group. Retrieved

January 10, 2006 (http://www.fbi.gov/hq/isd/cirg/tact.htm).

"Hostage Rescue Team." Wikipedia.com. Retrieved January 10, 2006 (http://www.reference.com/browse/wiki/Hostage_Rescue_Team).

International Association of Chiefs of Police and the Federal Law Enforcement Training Center. "Hostage Negotiation Study Guide 2003." Retrieved January 10, 2006 (http://www.learning-forlife.org/exploring/lawenforcement/study/hostage.pdf).

Johnson, Leroy. "Hostage Rescue and the Art of Negotiation." *Hostage Rescue Manual.* Revised edition. London, England: Greenhill Books, 2005. Retrieved January 10, 2006 (http://fm.greenhillbooks.com/greenhill/gbn/108/Hostage_rescue.html).

Macko, Steve. "*Hostage Rescue Team.*" Emergency Response & Research Institute. Retrieved January 2, 2006 (http://emernet.emergency.com/fbihost.htm).

Operational Tactics. Retrieved January 6, 2006. (http://www.operationaltactics.org).

Whitcomb, Christopher. *Cold Zero.* Clayton, Victoria, Australia: Warner Books, 2002.

Index

B
background check, 43
bank robbery, 4, 38, 41
bargaining chip, 7, 40
barricade, 4, 15, 16, 29, 49, 53
Bureau of Alcohol, Tobacco, and Firearms, 45

C
Central Intelligence Agency (CIA), 9
correctional settings, 23
counterterrorism, 13, 16, 17
Critical Incident Response Group (CIRG), 12–13

D
Delta Force, 14, 16

E
escape route, 41, 44

F
Federal Bureau of Investigation (FBI)
founding of CIRG, 12–13
headquarters, 13, 35
motto, 12
number of offices, 11
original hostage rescue team, 12
purpose of, 11
requirements, 35

G
Group d'Intervention de la Gendarmerie Nationale (GIGN), 14

H
helicopter, 15, 30
hostage crisis, stages of, 41–44
hostage negotiator
definition of, 4–5, 16, 25

Index

duties, 5, 6, 13, 14, 15–16, 24, 39
employers of, 9, 18, 21
equipment used, 14, 26–30
funding for, 11
skills, 10, 22, 25, 29, 34, 36, 37
techniques, 20, 25, 33, 38, 41, 46–47, 49–51
training, 5, 11, 13, 16, 18, 21, 23, 25, 26, 33, 34, 36, 37, 38

hostage taker
emotional state, 4, 7, 23–24, 25, 34, 36, 42, 44, 47
identity of, 4, 18, 39
motivations, 6–7, 24, 39–40, 41, 43
tactics, 6, 7, 8, 20, 23

human shield, 40

I

international hostage rescue, 16–18

J

jumpers, negotiating with, 23–24

M

manhunt, 15

O

Olympic Games, 12, 16
Operations Training Unit (OTU), 13–14

P

provisions, 23
psychology, 5, 16, 20, 36, 44, 46, 47
Public Agency Training Council, 21

R

raid, 16, 18, 45
risk assessment, 22, 24–25

S

Secret Service, 9
sniper rifle, 26, 28
Special Forces, 13, 14, 16, 18, 19
special response team (SRT), 9, 10, 11
standoff, 4, 31, 47
SWAT, 4, 9, 30, 36, 49

T

tear gas, 27, 29, 52
terrorists, 7, 11, 14, 15, 18, 39

W

weapons, used by hostage rescuers, 28–29

About the Author

Jamie Poolos has written a number of books for young adults including the award-winning *Inside Special Operations: The U.S. Army Rangers* and *Terrorist Attacks: The Tokyo Subway Attack*. He lives in California.

Photo Credits

Cover © LM Otero/AP/Wide World Photos; p. 5 © Bob Shaw/AP/Wide World; p. 8 © Amy Sinisterra/AP/Wide World; p. 10 © Scott McCloskey/AP/Wide World; pp. 12, 42 © Bettmann/Corbis; p. 15 Getty Images; p. 17 © Ivan Sekretarev/AP/Wide World; p. 21 © Jim Michaud/AP/Wide World; p. 24 © Patrick Chauvel/Sygma/Corbis; p. 27 © Joe Appel/AP/Wide World; p. 30 © Thanassis Stavrakis/AP/Wide World; p. 32 © Tom Hood/AP/Wide World; pp. 35, 37 © Anna Clopet/Corbis; p. 40 © Tim Roske/AP/Wide World; p. 45 © Susan Weems/AP/Wide World; p. 48 © Ted S. Warren/AP/Wide World; p. 52 © Maxim Marmur/AP/Wide World.

Editor: Joann Jovinelly

Date Due

SEP 14 '10			
DEC 02			
JAN 05			
JAN 19			
FEB 01			
OCT 10			
JAN 12			
SEP 29			
OCT 16			
JAN 25			
NOV 25			

BRODART, CO.   Cat. No. 23-233   Printed in U.S.A.